Daybreak
Gaining Strength Through Our Pain

Day-to-Day Encouragement

Poems by

Angela Y. Hodge

Mani Publishing, llc
Barbara Joe Williams
Tallahassee, Florida

Copyright © 2011by: Angela Y. Hodge
All rights reserved. No part of this book may be reproduced in any form without the expressed written permission of the publisher, except by a reviewer. All Scriptures are from the New King James version of the Bible.

Amani Publishing, LLC
P. O. Box 12045
Tallahassee, FL 32317
(850) 264-3341

A company based on faith, hope, and love

Website: **www.barbarajoewilliams.com**

Email: **www.amanipublishing@aol.com**

ISBN: 9780981584799

LCCN: 2011938624

Cover photo courtesy of: **iStockPhoto.com**

Cover creation by: **Diane Bass**, TDB811@aol.com

Dedication

This book is dedicated to my children:
Tamika, Shantrelle, and Jalon.
Thank you for your inspirations.

To my grandchildren:
Shamya, Jamaal Jr., Jamauri, Jacoby, and Jameia
Thank you for all your love.

My son-in-law:
Jamaal
Thank you for your support.

*And now little children,
abide in Him, that when He appears,
we may have confidence and
not be ashamed before Him at His coming.
If you know that He is righteous,
you know that everyone who practices
righteousness is born of Him.*

- 1 John 2:28-29

Acknowledgements

I would first like to acknowledge the Father, Son, and Holy Ghost for loving and protecting me.

I thank God for His grace, mercy, and unconditional love that gave me the strength to stand strong.

I acknowledge my family:
My children, Tamika, Shantrelle, and Jalon
My grandchildren, Shamya, Jamaal Jr., Jamauri, Jacoby, and Jameia
My son-in-law, Jamaal
My parents, Richard & Mary Anderson
My brother-in-law and sister, Russell & Theresa Smith
Thanks to all of you for sharing your love as I travel this journey.
To all my nieces and nephews, thanks for believing in me.

I would like to give a heartfelt thanks to my church family:
Celebrate New Life Tabernacle, www.cnlt.org
To One Accord Prayer Ministry, thanks!

And to all of my family, friends, and colleagues who had faith in me and stood by me through it all, I thank you all as well.

Special thanks to:
Barbara Joe Williams, thanks for your guidance and leadership.
Marvin (Merv) Mattair, thanks for sharing in on my vision.
Gladys Roann, thank you for your continued support.
Diann Douglas, thank you for your heartwarming love.
The Tallahassee Authors Network members, thank you all.

And to the members of the Beautiful Blessed Sisters Book Club (BBSBC), I thank you all.

Introduction

*Delight yourself also in the Lord,
and He shall give you the desires of your heart.*

-Psalm 37:4

Daybreak: Gaining Strength Through Our Pain is a collection of poetry that I have written based on my journey of life: a life full of rejections, misunderstandings, illnesses, and trials.

Through my life lessons, I've learned how to pray, hold on, and call on the name of Jesus. I knew God had a purpose and a plan for me while I went through the battles, but when I realized my purpose in life... I begin to live.

I pray that *Daybreak: Gaining Strength Through Our Pain* will inspire you to keep the faith, to keep believing, and trusting Him, and enjoying the beauty life brings.

According to the dictionary, daybreak is the first appearance of daylight in the morning, so each day we need a *Daybreak* to help us through the day. And for the next thirty-one days, I hope this book will give you the encouragement needed to really begin living the life you want to live.

Don't give up on God, rest in, and wait patiently for Him.

Daybreak
Gaining Strength Through Our Pain

It's at the break of day; I observe a new dawn and a new horizon.
In my daybreak, I gain strength to live,
and realize that I have been set free.
This day, will be the day of new beginnings;
This day, is going to be a blessed day.

Through great expectations on this day, Father God:
I expect Your blessings and favor over me;
I expect Your healing in my life;
And, I expect Your protection over my family and I.

On this day, Father God, I will seek You;
my heart and soul long for You.
I will walk in total victory,
for You are protecting me from my enemies.
I will meditate fully within my heart.
I will receive Your love and believe in Your power.
I will smile and rejoice because I know that by placing
ALL my trust in You, Lord,
You will take great care of me!

Today, I WILL LIVE!
My friends, it's time for a DAYBREAK.

Table of Contents

Day 1	Be Encouraged
Day 2	Hold On
Day 3	Trust God
Day 4	Believe
Day 5	Let Your Light Shine
Day 6	Shout For Joy
Day 7	You've Got the Victory
Day 8	Don't Give Up
Day 9	Praise Him
Day 10	Smile
Day 11	Life Is Good
Day 12	Wisdom
Day 13	There Is Hope
Day14	Humbleness
Day 15	Kindness
Day 16	Blessings
Day 17	Strength
Day 18	I Am Special
Day 19	Prayer Changes Things
Day 20	A Change Will Come
Day 21	Love
Day 22	Be Strong
Day 23	Abide in Him
Day 24	Embrace Life
Day 25	It's All Working For My Good
Day 26	It Is Well With My Soul
Day 27	Joy
Day 28	Give Thanks
Day 29	Forgive
Day 30	Obey His Voice
Day 31	The Day of Healing

Day 1

Be Encouraged

Encourage—
to inspire with courage, spirit,
or confidence to give support.

*Trust in the Lord with all your heart,
and lean not on you own understanding;
in all your ways acknowledge him,
and he shall direct your paths.*

- Proverbs 3:5-6

Be Encouraged

Smile! It will work for your good.
Rejoice! For it will be alright.

Don't let pains from your past hold you down.
Lift your head and BE ENCOURAGED!

You can make it; you can stand, keep the faith,
and keep standing strong.
Speak life and you soon will see how the Lord will deliver you.
BE ENCOURAGED.

It's through our pain, that we gain strength to live, to be free,
to be happy, and victorious.
So smile and give Him praise! There will be a brighter day!
He died so we can live; BE ENCOURAGED.

Let your love flow for others. Let your bonds stay strong.
Speak kindness to others, and rebuild the trust.
Let go of past hurt and let forgiveness take a stand,
For forgiveness will set you free.

Open your heart to love past all the rejection.
Open your mind to receive the joy.
There is nothing too hard for God to do;
be not dismayed.

He will strengthen you; He will help you!
BE ENCOURAGED!

Day 2

Hold On

*Hear my cry, O God,
attend unto my prayer,
from the end of the earth I will cry to you,
when my heart is overwhelmed,
lead me to the rock that is higher than I.*

- Psalm 61

The Battle That Was Within Me

Often times, I wondered where it all went wrong.
I was in a shell, feeling like I was alone in this big world.
I cried out loud, but no one seemed to hear me.

Through the pain, lies, and abuse I endured, I built a shell for myself.
I held on to the past. Pain, hate, and unforgiveness were a part of me.
On the outside, I laughed and smiled,
while no one knew there was a cry within me.

Hate and unforgiveness became my friends.
I held them close, not knowing they could destroy me.
I went to church and prayed often,
hoping one day that this cry would end.

This cry seemed so small, yet, it was tearing me apart.
Day by day, I felt my life melting away.

I wanted to be accepted by friends and family.
I looked for love in all the wrong places.
I wondered, "Where do I belong?"
and "Who do I belong to?"

As the nights came,
my tears watered the soft pillows that rested my head.
I constantly tossed and turned through the nights,
as I was disturbed by this battle within me.

Just when I thought all hope was gone,
I was confronted by a dream.
I was given a choice:
Will I survive this battle or stay in this shell?

There were so many things that rambled through my mind.
But, who could I depend on, to dry my tears and heal the depression?

I had known of this man named JESUS,
and I called on Him to help me through the hurt, heartache,
and pain.

Lord, I NEED HELP! I just want to be happy and free.
When I look into the mirror, I see a beautiful, but sad Black woman,
who seeks hope, joy, and happiness.
Where can I find peace?
Peace that calms this pain I feel inside,
peace that releases me from this shell,
peace that makes me smile again?
Lord, don't let bitterness or envy reside in me.
Show me how to forgive,
so I can be set free from this battle within me.
I surrender all to you!

Oh, on that day, I surrendered all.
JESUS came in and forgave me!
He put love where there was hate, joy where there was hurt,
and laughter where there was pain.
The cry I cried was no longer out of sadness and depression.
I took a stand and said,
NO MORE!
I'm taking back everything the devil has stolen from me!

I gained strength and power from His Holy word.
My happiness was returned to me!

Now, I am free! I am happy!
Best of all,
I am forgiven from the battle that was within me!

Day 3

Trust God

*The Lord is good to all;
and His tender mercies are over all His works.
All thy works shall praise you, O Lord;
and Your saints shall bless thee.
They shall speak of the glory of Your Kingdom,
and talk of Your power.*

- Psalm 145:9-11

Lord, Your Power is Real

Lord, Your power is real;
Your word is true. Why?
Is it that, when it comes to others,
we have the faith that You can move,
but when it is our time,
we question Your power or want You to prove?

My friends, life is good and full of adventures.
It's evident when we see the rain that pours from His sky,
When we feel the wind that blows fresh air,
When we see the beauty of the earth,
And when we observe the colors of hope, love and peace;
It shows His power is real.

Now, faith is being sure of what we hope for
and certain of the things we can't see.
You must have belief and assurance in Him,
to make it through and stand through the tests and pain.
Keep the Strength!

When the storms seem too hard to bear and you are at the end,
remember the things He's done for you
that may not have made sense at the time,
but worked out for your good.
Pull out the word you've hidden in your heart;
speak life, and know you belong to the King!
The power that lies in us is real.

When you surrender your life to Jesus,
you begin to feel a sense of hope, newness,
and amazement. His power is real.

When you're down in the valley in life,
remember you must believe in yourself.
It's in the valley you grow.

For all things work for the good;
we must not lose heart, nor give up.

Look at Jesus' journey:
He was betrayed, beaten, spit on, lied on,
and nailed to the cross for your sins and mine,
but the reward came on the third day
because He rose with all power in His hand.

And, for this I say,
"Lord, your power is real!"

Day 4

Believe

*For His merciful kindness is great toward us,
and the truth of the Lord,
endures forever.*

- Psalm 117:2

A Second Chance

The Love of God helps me endure many circumstances in life.
The Hope of God helps me embrace life's challenges with
pride and contentment.
The Faith of God helps me speak life over all battles
and walk in victory.
The Peace of God helps me rest in His care,
knowing everything will be alright.

The Grace of God helped me release all fears
and doubts that came from all my unbelief.
The Power of God gave me strength to gain authority
back over my life.
The Mercy of God gave me new life
and a second chance.

Day 5

Let Your Light Shine

The Lord is my light and my salvation;
whom shall I fear?
The Lord is the strength of my life;
of whom shall I be afraid?

- Psalm 27:1

The Light

Dear God:

Thank you for the light that gave light to me.

Thank you for the light that gave me hope.

When I felt I couldn't go on,
oppressed by the fear of being hurt over again,
a wall began to build.

But, in the midst of all the dark and lonely nights,
there was a small light that gave me great light.

Thank you, Lord,
for I know you are the light of the world,
and that You shine Your light,
so that I may see rays of sunshine
in the beauty it brings.

Thank you, Lord!

In Jesus' name,
Amen!

Day 6

Shout For Joy

*Do not sorrow,
for the joy of the Lord
is your strength.*

- Nehemiah 8:10

The Joy That Floods My Soul

To know the joy it brings when you've survived that test.
When you rose above the storm,
you were given relief and assurance,
knowing you came out on top.

To know the joy it brings when you were freed from bondage,
and you stood tall,
letting go of the things that kept you in total captivity.

To know the joy it brings when your rainy nights
turned to sunshiny days;
when you released the weights, one by one,
that used to easily upset you,
and you began to leap and reach for the stars.

To know the joy it brings when you've tried everything else
and they ALL failed,
but you tried Jesus,
and He gave you victory that comes when you live
according to His purpose for your life . . .

THAT'S THE JOY THAT FLOODS MY SOUL!

Day 7

You've Got the Victory

*Therefore take up the whole armor of God,
that you may be able to withstand
in the evil day
and having done all to stand.*

- Ephesians 6:13

Courage

We must have the courage to forgive;
We must have the faith to believe.
We must have the power to live,
for life and death lies in the power of the tongue.

Speak over yourself; speak life back into your body.
Sickness will not defeat you; pain will not destroy you.
Have the courage to dig beneath the surface
and pull out the faith and love you'll need,
to survive this test.

Courage is brave and will pass a test,
but remember who your God is;
let Him lead the way.
Acknowledge Him, for He will direct your path.

In every situation, there is a lesson to learn.
Ask God, "Lord, what are you trying to teach me?"
But, when He answers, be willing to let go of it all,
For when we hold on to mess and foolishness,
it corrupts the spirit of man.

KEEP THE COURAGE!

My friends, God is looking for bold soldiers,
who are strong and mighty in power.
Read His word daily and gain strength and power.
If you want more knowledge, it's in His Word.
If you want more understanding, it's in His Word.
If you want more peace, it's in His Word.
If you want the Fruits of the Spirit to increase and
operate fully in you, it's in His Word!
Take the time to learn and do more in Him
and your COURAGE will stand tall.

Day 8

Don't Give Up

But he who endures to the end shall be saved.

- Matthew 24:13

Don't Give Up

Don't give up;
Don't give in.
Hold on to your faith and pray.
Your life has just begun.

Trust in the Lord.
Wait patiently for Him.
Don't give up;
Don't give in.

The race is already won.
Don't give up;
Don't give in.

Day 9

Praise Him

*And the things that you have heard
from me among many witnesses,
commit these to faithful men
who will be able to teach others also.
You, therefore, must endure hardship
as a good soldier of Jesus Christ.*

- 2 Timothy 2:2-3

Surrender
(Dedicated to Jermonica Davis)

Down in the depths, my soul cried out.
In the midst of my pain
and disappointments, my soul cried out.
In the midst of rejection, my soul cried out.
In the midst of shame and guilt, my soul cried out.

I prayed and cried, cried and prayed.
Lord, I surrender.

It's through my pain that I gain strength.
Trials come to make me strong,
but a growth of maturity and a character must be born.
I yield my all to You; this battle is too hard for me to fight.
I raise my hands to you and surrender.
I have given it all to you: my cares, my hurt, and my tears,
for the steps of a good man are ordered by the Lord.

Lord, help me to run to peace and find comfort in understanding.
I can't hold on to the things that will pull me down.
I can't change man, but I can change me!
It's not what a person does or has done to me;
it's what I do that I will have to give an account for.
I surrender.

I will embrace life and see the beauty of today;
help me not to say anything hurtful.
I surrender to God and not my current circumstances.

I speak life!
I speak blessings!
I speak prosperity!

Lord, I surrender.

Day 10

Smile

You will show me the path of life;
In Your presence is fullness of joy;
At your right hand
are pleasures forevermore

- Psalm 16:11

No More Tears

You don't have to cry anymore;
Jesus knows your pain.

You don't have to cry anymore;
in Him, you will gain.

No More Tears!

Speak to the mountain that is holding you down.

Cast your cares on Him.

Keep the faith and don't give in.

You can make it, you can stand tall.
Jesus died, for us all!

Trust in Him to bring you through.

Believe in Him and you will have power.

Speak life, rise, and be made whole again.

NO MORE TEARS!

Day 11

Life Is Good

*For I know that my redeemer lives,
and He shall stand at last on the Earth.*

- Job 19:25

Your Redeemer Lives

Have you ever been in that trial that seems like there is no ending?

That trial that had you so consumed that you shut yourself
from the world;
That trial that had you questioning everything you ever
knew about God;
That trial that locked your lips from giving God the praise;
That trial that held you hostage in the comfort of your home;
That trial that beat you with shame and made you want to give up;
That trial that made you hurt so badly,
that anger and bitterness became your best friend?

Well, in the midst of your deepest fear,
embrace that trial with confidence
and know who you are in Christ Jesus!
Weeping may endure for a night,
but joy comes in the morning.

It was those trials that made you stronger!
For every trial we face,
there is a new level of growth we obtain!

And with this, know, without a shadow of a doubt,
that your redeemer lives.

Day 12

Wisdom

Get wisdom!
Get understanding!
Forget it not,
neither decline from
the words of my mouth.
Do not forsake her,
and she will preserve you;
love her, and she will keep you.
Wisdom is the principal thing,
Therefore, get wisdom,
and in all thy getting,
get understanding.

- Proverbs 4:5-7

Don't Give Up On Your Dream

All so long ago, I had my dream inside.
There were so many changes and mistakes,
but my dream stayed alive.

Where is my dream that laid so close to my heart?
Where is the passion that once filled my soul?

Can I rise and take the stand?

Sure you can!
You may dream of being a teacher,
a nurse, a doctor, or lawyer?

Don't give up nor give in.
Hold onto your dream.

Work hard and study;
Sow a seed to education.

Believe in yourself;
Love yourself deep inside your heart.

Your dream will come forth
and you will prosper.

Day 13

There Is Hope

*Beloved,
I pray that you may prosper in
ALL things and be in health,
just as your soul prospers.*

- 3 John 1:2

The Healing Prayer

Father God, in the Name of Jesus,
Thank you for this day, for this is the day that You,
Lord, have made,
I will rejoice and be glad in it.

Please forgive me for all my sins;
help me to forgive others so my healing can begin.

Lord, You are my healer.
You are the strength of my life;
my soul cries out for healing.

Heal my mind, so I'll think of You.
Heal my body, so I can walk in victory.
Heal my eyes,
so I can look beyond the faults of man
and see his needs.
Heal my ears from gossip and mischief.

Hear my cry, Oh Lord;
Rescue me and heal me.

In Jesus' name,
Amen!

Day 14

Humbleness

*But the fruit of the Spirit is love,
joy, peace, forbearance, kindness, goodness,
faithfulness, gentleness, and self control.
Against such things there is no law.*

- Galatians 5:22-23

∞

There Is a Lesson to Learn

For every breath we take,
there is a lesson to learn,
a task to master,
and a trial to overcome.
Deep inside, there is a voice of hope,
a smile of reassurance;
Yes, there is a lesson to learn.

Let your love have her perfect work;
let your faith take her stand.
And, oh, don't forget the peace that makes it alright.
There is a lesson to learn in this journey of life.

In this lesson to learn,
make your day count.
Hold on to your joy.
Maintain your self-control.
Fear not of longsuffering,
but stay humble and happy.

Love your enemies.
Pray for those who spitefully use you.
Forgive and be forgiven.
Yes, there is a lesson to learn.

Once you've mastered the lesson and passed the test,
You'll be free from sin and an overcomer of fear.

Oh, how I give Him praise!

Take a stand and keep the faith.
God knows the thoughts and plans that He has for you.

There is a lesson to learn in all we do!

Day 15

Kindness

*Beloved,
let us love one another,
for love is of God.
Everyone who loves
is born of God
and knows God.*

- 1 John 4:7

∞

The Puzzle

We are all pieces of a united puzzle,
There is a place where we each connect,
and a place where we link.

Together, the puzzle should be mended,
but there are special pieces that have to be formed.

When our pieces are ready and shaped to fit,
our puzzle will connect and be born again.

I'll give the smile,
you give the hug,
and when we are mended together,
we'll both be able to stand.

Love ye, one another and be true;
For there is a piece of the puzzle inside of you.

Day 16

Blessings

*Train up a child in the way he should go,
and when he is old he will not depart from it.*

- Proverbs 22:6

∞

The Love of a Mother
(Dedicated to My Children)

What is a great mother?
Sure, she's the one who calms the cries, fixes the wounds,
and prepares the meals, but let's not forget, she teaches the lessons.
She teaches her kids how to love, keep God first, repent of their sins,
and keep their faith.

Motherhood is a ministry, a task that must be done,
but sometimes, the road gets long and weary.

I used to find myself asking,
"Lord, I need direction.
Is there a map I can follow or a compass that can direct my path?
I need your help traveling this journey.
Enhance my motherhood, Lord,
Show me how to train, encourage, discipline, and embrace my kids."

It was in the Bible, where I found answers to my daily needs
and the tools I needed to build on the foundation.

Just take the time to read it; you've got to have a plan and a vision.

A good mother, yes, that's what I am striving to be:
One who is there,
One who listens,
One who shields and protects,
One who loves with affection,
And, one who will take a stand for what is right.

Tamika, Shantrelle, and Jalon,
I LOVE YOU!

I am truly thankful for the gift of being a MOTHER.

Day 17

Strength

*He gives the power to the weak,
and to those who have no might,
He increases strength.*

- Isaiah 40:29

∞

Prayer For Strength

Dear God:
Thank You for allowing me to see another day.
Please forgive me for all my sins;
Create in me a clean heart
and renew the right spirit within me.

Please don't let bitterness or anger be a part of me.
Help me to acknowledge my faults
and seek Your presence for restoring and rebuilding.

Thank You for answering prayer and giving me another chance.
You are able to do just what You said You would do.
Thank You for Your love, peace, and grace that renew me each day.

Lord, you see and know all.
STRENGTH is what I need today,
for there is nothing too hard for You to do.

In Your word, you state,
"I can do all things through Christ who strengthens me,"
and when I feel weak, that's when I am strong.
I am trusting in You for strength and power.

In Jesus' name,
Amen!

Day 18

I Am Special

For you formed my inward parts;
You covered me in my mother's womb.
I will praise You,
for I am fearfully and wonderfully made,
marvelous are Your works,
and that my soul knows very well.

- Psalm 139:13-14

∞

Fearfully and Wonderfully Made

From the womb, He knew me.
By name, He called me.
Trials and disappointment
taught me how to pray and how to stand.
Yes, I was fearfully and wonderfully made.

When He created me,
He gave me valuable traits:
My eyes, to see the beauty of the world,
My head, so I may think of Christ,
My ears, to hear the Word of God,
And, my nose,
to smell the flowers with the beauty they bring,

He gave me my mouth to speak wisdom,
My hands, to give Him praise,
My heart, to love my neighbor,
just as I love myself,
My legs, to walk in victory,
And, my feet to dance in triumph.

Fearfully and wonderfully made,
I am unique.
Special and loved,
Jesus took the time to make everything right.

I will praise Him for all He has done.
He washed my soul and made me whole.

Oh, there will never be another like me,
I was FEARFULLY AND WONDERFULLY made!

Day 19

Prayer Changes Things

*Therefore, as the elect of God,
holy and beloved,
put on tender mercies,
kindness, humility,
meekness, longsuffering;
Bearing with one another,
and forgiving one another,
if anyone has a complaint against another:
even as Christ forgave you,
so you also must do.*

- Colossians 3:12-13

∞

The Memories
(Dedicated to My Family & Friends)

Bad memories lay quietly on the surface,
trying hard to be remembered,
but I overcame evil by doing good works.
Some days,
those bad memories would overshadow my thoughts.

I remember those bad memories of abuse
that I tried to tuck away;
Being scared by the battle that lied within me,
Living through days of sorrow and nights of terror,
Those were the memories that seemed to last forever.

But, I captured those bad memories with a ray of hope.
I turned those bad memories into good testimonies,
And now, I stand on truth, trust in God's word,
and remind Him of His promises.

To my children, grandchildren, family, and friends:

Don't let bad memories hold you in captivity
because at the end,
God is greater than any problem
or trial that may arise in your lives.

He restored me from fear and doubt
and He gave me a second chance.
If he did it for me,
He will do the same for you.

Day 20

A Change Will Come

*Through whom also we have access
by faith into this grace,
in which we stand,
and rejoice in hope of the Glory of God.
And not only that,
we also glory in tribulations,
knowing that tribulation produces perseverance;
perseverance [produces] character;
and character [produces] hope.*

- Romans 5:2-4

∞

The Untold Story

Who would have ever known the story that's never been told,
about the character that has to be born?
In the heart of the soul,
there is an untold story waiting to be born.

At the start of my life's journey, my story began.
As I became older, many questioned my faith in God
and others mocked my belief.
But, deep down, there was a story waiting to be reborn.

They didn't know my story;
they didn't know what I had been through.
Yet, they judged me, separated themselves from me,
and again, questioned my faith in God.
I stood through the shame, in meekness and humility,
but this was where the untold story of mine was transformed.

I realized that I had to believe in myself and build my confidence in
GOD, for He is the light of my salvation,
and He will bless the righteous with favor.

I knew there was a purpose for all I'd gone through.
Our testimonies bring change, our faith brings blessings,
and our wisdom brings mercy.

The untold story has so many gifts,
Oh, what power it is that lies within.

My friends,
Your story lies within you.
Hold on to your story and keep the faith.
Your story will make a difference in someone's life.
Some people may never know your untold story,
but put your trust in God and let Him lead the way.

Day 21

Love

*Love suffers long and is kind;
love does not envy;
love does not parade itself,
is not puffed up;
does not behave rudely,
does not seek its own,
is not provoked,
thinks no evil;
does not rejoice in iniquity
but rejoices in the truth.*

-1 Corinthians 13:4-6

∞

The Heart of Love

The heart of love brings the most beautiful words
into a garden of hope.

From one side of happiness, to the other with joy,
the heart utters the most profound beat.

The heart of love that is full of hope, humbleness,
and kindness, is built up on faith and restored by grace.

So, smile and be merry; clap and be blessed.

Hand all your problems to Jesus, for He cares.

Enter into His presence with thanksgiving.

Admit your faults and be forgiven.

Rest in His arms; know that He is near.

Trust in Him to make everything alright.

The Heart of Love…let it flow.

Day 22

Be Strong

*Show me Your ways,
O Lord, teach me Your paths.
Lead me in Your truth and teach me,
for You are the God of my salvation;
on You I wait all the day.*

-Psalm 25:4-5

∞

This Heart of Mine

Lord, my heart is hurting; the pain is unbearable.
My soul needs a revival; the rain is pouring.

Will the sun ever shine again?
"Oh, Yes!"
Deep inside, the voice of hope says it will.

It's through your pain where you gain strength.
It's through your heartache where you gain power
power to love again,
power to stand,
and power to endure.

Lord, I know You are watching.
I know in every situation,
there is a lesson to learn, a task to master,
and a battle to win.
I will survive; I will not quit!

The heart is a shelter for the soul.
It's a protector, a comforter,
and it utters the most powerful words, feelings, and needs.

Lord, help me, hold me, and guide me.
If my heart leaks, I lose happiness, laughter, and joy.
Seal it, so it can transform:
My pain to love,
My sadness to joy, and
My confusion to clarity.

Yes, my heart, Lord,
heal THIS HEART OF MINE.

Day 23

Abide in Him

*If you abide in me
and my words abide in you,
you will ask what you desire,
and it shall be done for you,
by this my Father is glorified,
that you bear much fruit;
so you will be my disciples.*

- **John 15:7-8**

∞

The True Vine

Dear God:

I will praise You in present circumstances.
I know You are the true vine,
so I ask that You cut off every branch in me that bears no fruit.
Cleanse me thoroughly and for every branch that does not bear fruit,
prune it, so it can be fruitful.

Prepare me for Your ministry.
Help me to see in the spiritual realm and not carnally.
When I focus on all the tasks and things on my agenda for today,
help me to invest time in studying your word and
grant me quiet time to rest in your presence.
Let my actions reflect your character as
I embrace honesty and self-control.

The tree is known by the fruit it bears.
I will bear good fruit:
The fruit of understanding,
The fruit of love,
The fruit of humility, and
The fruit of giving.
In Jesus' Name,
Amen!

Day 24

Embrace Life

*Jesus said to her,
"I am the resurrection and the life.
He who believes in me,
though he may die,
he shall live,
and whoever lives and
believes in me shall never die."
Do you believe this?*

- John 11:25-26

∞

The Miracle That Was Unfolded
(Dedicated to my niece, Rashonta Mashay Hall)

Oh, on the day of September 12, 1992, my niece, Rashonta, was
born, weighing only 1 pound, 14 ounces.
As she came into the world, her face was blue and purple,
due to a lack of oxygen.
She was so tiny; I could hold her whole body in my hand.
Every breath she took could have been her last one,
but she fought to hold on, she fought to LIVE.

God has a purpose and a plan, and what God has for you,
is for YOU!

Tallahassee Memorial Hospital
became her home for the next three months.
I remember my heart skipping beats when my phone rang,
leaving me wondering if that was the call with the bad news
about her fight.

We traveled many miles, went up and down many elevators,
two and three days a week, just to see our little angel who had
a will to live.

There were so many questions left unanswered and
so many medical terms thrown at us,
but we kept the faith.
The doctors would say,
"We don't know the outcome, or what lies ahead,
but we will take it one day at a time."

Things began to look up again, but to our surprise,
she had to be rushed to surgery to open her heart valves.
The clock ticked, and hours passed by,
but we were relieved when the doctor came to assure us
that everything went well.

From then, days seemed like weeks, weeks seemed like months,
but she kept the strength and fought a good fight.
With every breath she took, every prayer we prayed,
He stepped in and healed her.
Now, we know there is nothing too hard for God to do.

Remember this:
When things seem hopeless and you don't feel you can stand,
think about the miracle that I held in my hand.

Our Little Angel, Rashonta, is now 19-years-old and a 2011 honors graduate of Madison County High School.

Don't give up on God!

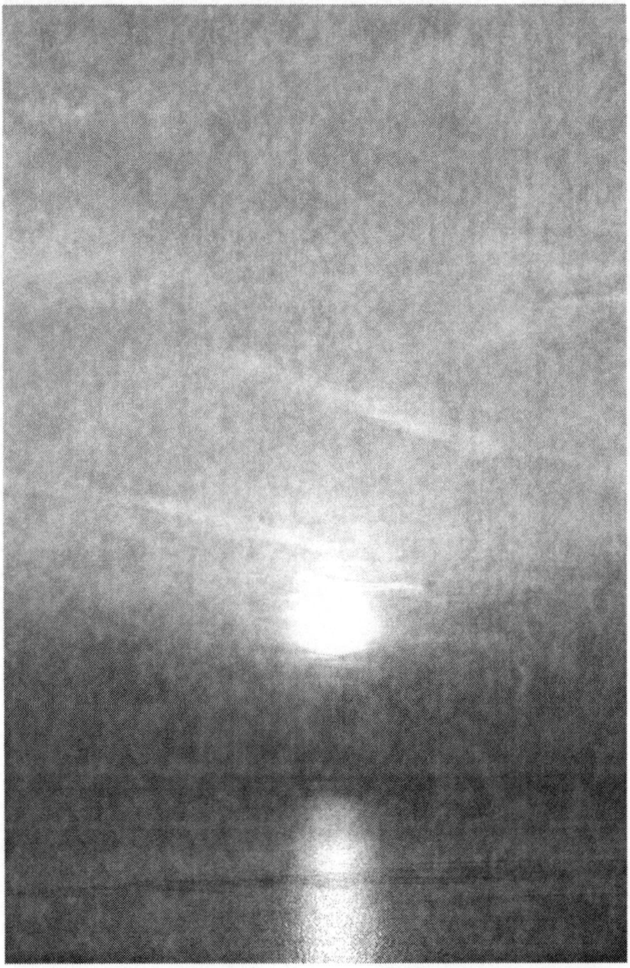

Day 25

It's All Working For My Good

*But now, O Lord,
are our Father;
we are the clay
and you are the potter;
we are all the work
of your hand.*

- Isaiah 64:8

∞

Empower

Father God, in the name of Jesus,
Hear my cry and incline unto me.

Restore unto me the joy of thy salvation;
Forgive me for my lack of trust.

Whenever I try to do right,
someone always seems to find fault in me:
In my appearance,
In the way I smile,
Even in the way I talk.

Lord, you created me;
You formed me.
Let me remain true to You and
know You have a plan for my life.

Protect me as I travel this journey.
Empower me to live in Your will and
submit to Your restoration process.

I will praise You in ALL circumstances;
I will call upon You and stand courageously.

Shine Your light on me and help me
to focus on Your kingdom,
so I may do Your will,
even when I don't understand
Your ultimate plan for my life.

Empower me to live in love and walk in victory.
In Jesus' Name,
Amen!

Day 26

It Is Well With My Soul

*A time to weep and a time to laugh,
a time to mourn and a time to dance.*

- Ecclesiastes 3:4

∞

The Rainbow

There is a rainbow amongst the soul
of every storm that crosses our paths.
We must keep the faith and know that
the sun will shine again.

I will dance in the rain;
I will dance through the pain.

What are the elements to the rainbow?
What is it about the rainbow that gives us hope
and comforts us with its special touch?

RAIN:

- The storms of life
- Trials and disappointments
- Hurt and pain
- Unforgiveness

COLORS:

- **Red** – The blood of Jesus that cleanses me and strengthens me daily.

- **Orange** – A mix of sickness mixed with the power of the blood. By His stripes, we are healed.

- **Yellow** – Sickness, which was defeated at the cross. I CAN be made whole again.

- **Green** – Immature and unskilled. Acknowledge Him in all thy ways and He will direct your path.

- **Blue** – Sadness, but He will wipe the tears from your eyes.

- **Purple** – Royal power. You shall receive power after the Holy Ghost has come upon you.

SUNSHINE:

- Courage
- Deliverance
- Faith
- Freedom
- Happiness
- Hope
- Humility
- Love
- Praise

Believe God and trust in His word.
Give a smile, give a hug.

Stand tall, share your rainbow, and let it glow;
It could save a life!

Day 27

Joy

These things I have spoken to you, that my joy may remain in you and that your joy may be full.

- John 15:11

∞

In Your Darkest Hour

When you feel you have no one,
listen to the small voice that whispers to you,
Don't give up.
Through all your challenges and darkest hours,
have confidence in God's promises,
He will embrace you with His love.

Lord,
in spite of all my inferiority, insecurity, and inadequacy,
You still gave me the confidence to believe in myself.
I can rise again!

It's in our darkest hours,
where God wants us to be in,
so He can purge and
cleanse us to make us whole again.

Seek the Lord and He will answer.
He will deliver you from all of your fears.

Put your trust in Him
and let Him lead the way.
He WILL give you LIGHT
in your darkest hour.

Day 28

Give Thanks

I will love you,
Oh Lord, my strength.
The lord is my rock and
my fortress and my deliverer;
my God,
my strength in whom I will trust,
my shield and the horn of my salvation,
my stronghold.

- Psalm 18:1-2

∞

Protection

Dear God:
Help me to always remember that You are my source and
when the enemy comes in like a flood,
Your Holy Spirit will lift up a standard.
I am thankful for all of the things You have done for me;
You brought me out of the miry clay.
And, for this, I am blessed.

The people you have placed in my circle,
let them be strong and of good faith,
holding on to Your promises daily.

Lord, I can't control what others do or say,
but in the midst of my going through,
help me to keep my eyes on You.
When the enemy tried to destroy me,
his weapon did not prosper.
I overcame that battle!

God, I know you can do exceedingly and
abundantly above all that I can ask or think.
You are my fortress, my shield, and buckler.
Hide me in a secret place.

I will call upon You, who is worthy of my praises.

A thousand may fall at thy right hand, but no evil will befall me.
Thank You for protecting me.
I see the growth and maturity that lies within.
You are mighty!

I give You honor, praise, and glory!
In Jesus' Name,
Amen!

Day 29

Forgive

*If my people,
who are called by my name,
will humble themselves and pray
and seek my face and
turn from their wicked ways,
then I will hear from heaven,
and will forgive their sin
and heal their land.*

- 2 Chronicles 7:14

∞

My President's Prayer
(Dedicated to the 44th President of the United States, Barack Obama)

Dear Lord:
Bless the President and keep a shield of protection around him.
Cover the White House, the First Lady, their children,
family, friends, and the staff. I plead the blood of Jesus.

Order his steps in Your word. Lead and guide him,
as You have given him authority to lead this country.

Lord, when he is feeling weak, give him added strength.
When he is feeling sad, give him joy that overflows
from the love of his children.
When he needs direction, give him wisdom,
knowledge, and understanding.

When he needs peace, comfort him with Your love.
And, Lord, when it seems like there is no hope for him,
remind him of the place from where You have brought him.
Romans 8:28 says,
All things work together for the good of them that loves You, to them who are called according to Your purpose.

Lord, we need his leadership in this tumultuous time.
Restore our hope and faith in You.
Have mercy on Your people; let the change begin within me.

We need Your power to let forgiveness take a stand.
Yes, a change has come!

We are trusting in Your word.

In Jesus' Name,
Amen.

Day 30

Obey His Voice

*Trust in Him at all times, you people;
pour out your hearts before Him.
God is a refuge for us.*

- Psalm 62:8

∞

Plant the Seeds

On the edge of bitterness, you vow to never trust again.
Don't swallow the disappointments, for that yields to a broken heart.

Don't ignore the sadness and store it in a box.
Things happen, but you must go on.

Plant the seeds that will grow in time, if nurtured faithfully.
I even had to plant seeds of my own
to cross over the bridge of disappointment.

Use these seeds in your life to help you make it through your trials:

- The Seed of **Wisdom** – Psalms 18:2

- The Seed of **Fulfillment** – Matthew 5:6

- The Seed of **Security** – Ephesians 1:13

I realized that when I planted my seeds,
I also had to let go of my situation and stay in His word.
The sadness was a part of my healing!

Plant your seeds on good ground;
it will bring forth blessings to you and others.

Day 31

The Day of Healing

*Bless the Lord, O my soul:
and all that is within me,
bless his holy name.
Bless the Lord, O my soul,
and forget not all his benefits:
Who forgives all your iniquities;
who heals all your diseases;
Who redeems your life from destruction;
who crowns you with loving kindness
and tender mercies.*

- Psalm 103: 1-4

∞

The Amazing Journey of Healing

Often times, I was faced with decisions. There were choices I had to make. No matter how hard it seemed, I knew deep down that I had to stand on truth and believe it would all work for my good. Many times, I had to stand alone. Some days, fear would overtake me. Standing was hard, yet I managed to make it.

Through all the shame, lies, and rejection, there was always a voice that would softly whisper to me, *It's through your pain that you gain strength*. But, where would my strength come from? After many sleepless nights, the answer came, *You gain strength from My word*.

It was in the Bible, I found hope, strength, and faith to endure the journey. It was there, in His word, that I found peace to press on. It was there, in His unchanging word, that I found joy to overcome all fiery darts. Yes, it was indeed there, in His loving word, that I found comfort in knowing that the Holy Ghost would lead and direct my path.

So many people questioned my belief and faith in God. There was indeed a purpose and a plan for my life. A greater and deeper character needed to be born. But oh, on a hot, summer day in June 1995, an illness hit me. I went back and forth to the doctor, and I had never been eager for visits with the doctor. During those visits, I would stare at the wall as I patiently waited for the results. Confused and worried, tears fell from my face, and as I sat there, I could hear the air conditioner rumbling like a mighty, rushing wind.

For two years, I went to get check-ups every three months. Three years after that, those check-ups became required every six months.
I was becoming burned-out from crying, but I still called on Jesus! I petitioned him, "Lord, it's in your hands and I trust you! Healing is what I need! Please restore my soul!" Little did I know, he had ALREADY stepped in, healed my body, and set me free!

All I needed was a little faith! Those check-ups were cancelled. Worthy is thy name; prayer does change things. I fasted, I prayed, I overcame that sickness, I survived that test. Still, some nights were cold and lonely. Some days I felt blue. My hair fell out in patches. My legs would swell in pain. But, each day, I held on, as I quoted my favorite Scripture to ease the tension:

I waited patiently for the Lord; and He inclined unto me, and heard my cry, He brought me up also out of the horrible pit, out of the miry clay, and set my foot upon a rock, and established my going.

- Psalm 40:1-2

∞

Dear Friends:

I say to you, forgive, so your healing can begin!

When we do not forgive, it blocks our blessings. Speak life over every adverse or challenging situation in your life! Hold on. Don't give up. When we become weak, it is important that we stand in the strength of the "Great I Am," who lives within us. Keep the faith!

When you activate your faith, though, do not waver or become double-minded. Remember that ALL things are possible through Christ Jesus. In total darkness, He will shine His light and give you the strength and ability to start over again!

He is our healer!

My Prayer

Make your request known to God.

Dear God:

_____

_____

_____

_____

_____

_____

_____

_____

_____

_____

_____

_____

_____

_____

_____

_____

In Jesus' Name,
Amen!

About the Author

Angela Yolanda Hodge was born and raised in the beautiful town of Madison, Florida. Over the years, she encountered many challenges, rejections, and disappointments, which led her to express how she felt on paper, hoping it would one day, be a blessing to others.

It was through her pain where she gained strength to live again, be free, and stay strong. Angela is a graduate of North Florida Community College. Formerly, a teacher with the Early Head Start Services, Angela has over ten years experience in teaching.

Angela's desire to teach was driven by her curiosity in Special Education when her niece, Rashonta, fought hard to live, despite being born prematurely and given a small percentage to live. Rashonta's survival gave Angela hope in life and a strong passion in believing in God.

Angela believes strongly that families are built on memories that last forever. Her motto is, "Prayer is the key, faith unlocks the door." Angela currently resides and works in Tallahassee, Florida. She is the mother of three children, five grandchildren, and one son-in-law. She's also a dedicated member of the Tallahassee Authors Network and the Beautifully Blessed Sisters Book Club.

To Contact Angela Y. Hodge:

- Email: angelayhodge@gmail.com

- Website: www.angelayhodge.com

- Facebook: Angela Yolanda Hodge

Mailing Address:
Author Angela Y. Hodge
3539 Apalachee Pkwy, 3-84
Tallahassee, Florida 32311